CREATIVE  TOUCHES™

Floor Finishes

ETC.

THE HOME DECORATING INSTITUTE®

COWLES
Creative Publishing

A Division of Cowles Enthusiast Media, Inc.

Copyright © 1996 Cowles Creative Publishing, Inc., formerly Cy DeCosse Inc.
5900 Green Oak Drive Minnetonka, Minnesota 55343 · 1-800-328-3895 · All rights reserved · Printed in U.S.A.
Cataloging-in-Publication Data can be found on page 64.

CONTENTS

Getting Started

Tools & Supplies
8

Preparing the Surface
10

Primers & Finishes
12

Water-based Paints & Stains
14

Finishes for Wood Floors

Resurfacing &
Refinishing Basics
19

Resurfacing &
Refinishing Supplies
20

Stained Floors
27

Aged & Distressed
Finishes
31

Decorative Painting on Finished Floors

Painted Designs on
Wood Floors
37

Nature-printed
Floor Designs
43

Faux Wood Grain
47

Faux Stone Tiles
53

Floor Cloths
57

Floor Finishes
ETC.

Floors are so much more than functional when they are finished tastefully and creatively. Lest we underestimate the decorative impact of floors in the home, imagine how difficult it would be even to move from room to room without seeing the floor. With every step we take, our eyes are focused on the floor underfoot or up ahead.

Resurfacing and refinishing can bring an old wood floor back to life, with finishing options that include stains, washes, and paint in any color imaginable. A less-than-perfect wood floor might be given an aged painted finish that is both durable and decorative.

For added splash, decorative painted designs may border a room or emphasize alternating squares in a parquet floor. Designs may be stenciled, stamped, or brushed onto finished floors. Faux tiles or a checked pattern can be painted on the floor for an all-over effect. Creatively painted floor cloths can be made in designs to accent any decor, from contemporary to country.

Guided by colorful photography and step-by-step instructions, discover many creative touches to renew the beauty of your floors.

GETTING STARTED

Tools & Supplies

TAPES

When painting, use tape to mask off any surrounding areas. Several brands are available, varying in the amount of tack, how well they release from the surface without damaging the base coat, and how long they can remain in place before removal. You may want to test the tape before applying it to the entire project. The edge of the tape should be sealed tightly to prevent seepage.

PAINT ROLLERS

Paint rollers are used to paint an area quickly with an even coat of paint. Roller pads, available in several nap thicknesses, are used in conjunction with roller frames. Use synthetic or lamb's wool roller pads to apply water-based paints.

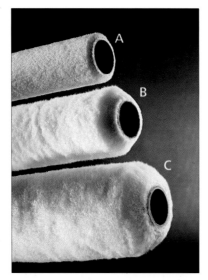

A. SHORT-NAP ROLLER PADS with 1/4" to 3/8" (6 mm to 1 cm) nap are used for applying glossy paints to smooth surfaces like wallboard, wood, and smooth plaster.

B. MEDIUM-NAP ROLLER PADS with 1/2" to 3/4" (1.3 to 2 cm) nap are used as all-purpose pads. They give flat surfaces a slight texture.

C. LONG-NAP ROLLER PADS with 1" to 1 1/4" (2.5 to 3.2 cm) nap are used to cover textured areas in fewer passes.

D. ROLLER FRAME is the metal arm and handle that holds the roller pad in place. A wire cage supports the pad in the middle. Select a roller frame with nylon bearings so it will roll smoothly and a threaded end on the handle so you can attach an extension pole.

E. EXTENSION POLE has a threaded end that screws into the handle of a roller frame. Use an extension pole when painting ceilings, high wall areas, and floors.

PAINTBRUSHES & APPLICATORS

Several types of paintbrushes and applicators are available, designed for various purposes. Select the correct one to achieve the best quality in the paint finish.

A. SYNTHETIC-BRISTLE paintbrushes are generally used with water-based latex and acrylic paints, while B. NATURAL-BRISTLE brushes are used with alkyd, or oil-based paints. Natural-bristle paintbrushes may be used with water-based paints to create certain decorative effects.

C. BRUSH COMBS remove dried or stubborn paint particles from paintbrushes and align the bristles so they dry properly. To use a brush comb, hold the brush in a stream of water as you pull the comb several times through the bristles from the base to the tips. Use mild soap on the brush, if necessary, and rinse well. The curved side of the tool can be used to remove paint from the roller pad.

Stencil brushes are available in a range of sizes. Use the small brushes for fine detail work in small stencil openings, and the large brushes for larger openings. Either D. SNYTHETIC or E. NATURAL-BRISTLE stencil brushes may be used with acrylic paints.

Artist's brushes are available in several types, including F. FAN, G. LINER, and H. FLAT BRUSHES. After cleaning the brushes, always reshape the head of the brush by stroking the bristles with your fingers. Store artist's brushes upright on their handles or lying flat so there is no pressure on the bristles.

I. SPONGE APPLICATORS are used for a smooth application of paint on flat surfaces.

J. PAINT EDGERS with guide wheels are used to apply paint next to moldings, ceilings, and corners. The guide wheels can be adjusted for proper alignment of the paint pad.

Preparing the Surface

To achieve a high-quality and long-lasting paint finish that adheres well to the surface, it is important to prepare the surface properly so it is clean and smooth. The preparation steps vary, depending on the type of surface you are painting. Often it is necessary to apply a primer to the surface before painting it. For more information about primers, refer to pages 12 and 13.

PREPARING SURFACES FOR PAINTING

SURFACE TO BE PAINTED	PREPARATION STEPS	PRIMER
UNFINISHED WOOD	1. Sand surface to smooth it. 2. Wipe with damp cloth to remove grit. 3. Apply primer.	Latex enamel undercoat.
PREVIOUSLY PAINTED WOOD	1. Clean surface to remove any grease and dirt. 2. Rinse with clear water; allow to dry. 3. Sand surface lightly to degloss and smooth it and to remove any loose paint chips. 4. Wipe with damp cloth to remove grit. 5. Apply primer to any areas of bare wood.	Not necessary, except to touch up areas of bare wood; then use latex enamel undercoat.
PREVIOUSLY VARNISHED WOOD	1. Clean surface to remove any grease and dirt. 2. Rinse with clear water; allow to dry. 3. Sand surface to degloss it. 4. Wipe with damp cloth to remove grit. 5. Apply primer.	Latex enamel undercoat.
UNFINSHED WALLBOARD	1. Dust with hand broom, or vacuum with soft brush attachment. 2. Apply primer.	Flat latex primer.
PREVIOUSLY PAINTED WALLBOARD	1. Clean surface to remove any grease and dirt. 2. Rinse with clear water; allow to dry. 3. Apply primer, only if making a dramatic color change.	Not necessary, except when painting over dark or strong color; then use flat latex primer.
UNPAINTED PLASTER	1. Sand any flat surfaces as necessary. 2. Dust with hand broom, or vacuum with soft brush attachment.	Polyvinyl acrylic primer.
PREVIOUSLY PAINTED PLASTER	1. Clean surface to remove any grease and dirt. 2. Rinse with clear water; allow to dry thoroughly. 3. Fill any cracks with spackling compound. 4. Sand surface to degloss it.	Not necessary, except when painting over dark or strong color; then use polyvinyl acrylic primer.
UNGLAZED POTTERY	1. Dust with brush, or vacuum with soft brush attachment. 2. Apply primer.	Polyvinyl acrylic primer or gesso.
GLAZED POTTERY, CERAMIC & GLASS	1. Clean surface to remove any grease and dirt. 2. Rinse with clear water; allow to dry thoroughly. 3. Apply primer.	Stain-killing primer.
METAL	1. Clean surface with vinegar or lacquer thinner to remove any grease and dirt. 2. Sand surface to degloss it and to remove any rust. 3. Wipe with damp cloth to remove grit. 4. Apply primer.	Rust-inhibiting latex metal primer.
FABRIC	1. Prewash fabric without fabric softener to remove any sizing, if fabric is washable. 2. Press fabric as necessary.	None.

Primers & Finishes

PRIMERS

Some surfaces must be coated with a primer before the paint is applied. Primers ensure good adhesion of paint and are used to seal porous surfaces so paint will spread smoothly without soaking in. It is usually not necessary to prime a nonporous surface in good condition, such as smooth, unchipped, previously painted wood or wallboard. Many types of water-based primers are available; select one that is suitable for the type of surface you are painting.

A

A. FLAT LATEX PRIMER is used for sealing unfinished wallboard. It makes the surface nonporous so fewer coats of paint are needed. This primer may also be used to seal previously painted wallboard before you apply new paint of a dramatically different color. The primer prevents the original color from showing through.

B

B. LATEX ENAMEL UNDERCOAT is used for priming most raw woods or woods that have been previously painted or stained. A wood primer closes the pores of the wood, for a smooth surface. It is not used for cedar, redwood, or plywoods that contain water-soluble dyes, because the dyes would bleed through the primer.

C. STAIN-KILLING PRIMER seals stains like crayon, ink, and grease so they will not bleed through the top coat of paint. It is used to seal knotholes and is the recommended primer for cedar, redwood, and plywood with water-soluble dyes. This versatile primer is also used for glossy surfaces like glazed pottery and ceramic, making it unnecessary to sand or degloss the surface.

C

FINISHES

Finishes are sometimes used over paint as the final coat. They protect the painted surface with a transparent coating. The degree of protection and durability varies, from a light application of matte aerosol sealer to a glossy layer of clear finish.

D. CLEAR FINISH, such as water-based urethanes and acrylics, may be used over painted finishes for added durability. Available in matte, satin, and gloss, these clear finishes are applied with a brush or sponge applicator. Environmentally safe clear finishes are available in pints, quarts, and gallons (0.5, 0.9, and 3.8 L) at paint supply stores and in 4-oz. and 8-oz. (119 and 237 mL) bottles or jars at craft stores.

E. AEROSOL CLEAR ACRYLIC SEALER, available in matte or gloss, may be used as the final coat over paint as a protective finish. A gloss sealer also adds sheen and depth to the painted finish for a more polished look. Apply aerosol sealer in several light coats rather than one heavy coat, to avoid dripping or puddling. To protect the environment, select an aerosol sealer that does not contain harmful propellants. Use all sealers in a well-ventilated area.

Water-based Paints & Stains

A wide variety of paint is available from paint supply stores and craft stores. Each type has advantages that make it especially suitable for certain kinds of painting. All of the following are water-based, making cleanup easy with soap and water. Water-based paints are also safer for the environment than oil-based paints.

LATEX PAINTS

Latex paint is fast drying and durable. In addition to the wide range of premixed colors, latex paint can be custom-mixed by a paint professional. It is available in various finishes, from flat latex for a matte appearance to high-gloss latex with maximum sheen. Low-luster latex enamel paint, sometimes referred to as eggshell enamel, has some sheen and provides good coverage; semigloss has a bit more sheen. The glossier the paint, the more durable it is. Packaged in pints, quarts, and gallons (0.5, 0.9, and 3.8 L), latex paint is suitable for general use in small and large jobs.

Latex paint contains acrylic or vinyl resins or a combination of both. Latex paints of acrylic resins are the highest quality, with vinyl-acrylic blends next in quality, followed by paints consisting solely of vinyl resins. High-quality paints may cost significantly more, but they provide an even, complete coverage and wear longer.

For durable painted floors, select an interior/exterior latex paint specifically designed for floors. Enamels are available in high-gloss or low-gloss finishes and some are formulated to resist dirt, stains, grease, and mildew. Some are also water repellent. Enamels can be applied to previously painted or varnished floors and to unfinished wood floors.

CRAFT ACRYLIC PAINT

Craft acrylic paint contains 100 percent acrylic resins. Generally sold in 2-oz., 4-oz., and 8-oz. (59, 119, and 237 mL) bottles or jars, these premixed acrylics have a creamy brushing consistency and give excellent coverage. They should not be confused with the thicker artist's acrylics used for canvas paintings. Craft acrylic paint can be diluted with water, acrylic extender, or latex paint conditioner if a thinner consistency is desired. Craft acrylic paints are available in many colors and in metallic, fluorescent, and iridescent formulas.

WATER-BASED WOOD STAINS

Water-based wood stains are available in a wide variety of natural wood tones as well as several colored tints. Because they are water-based, they are also quick-drying, easy to use, and safe for the environment.

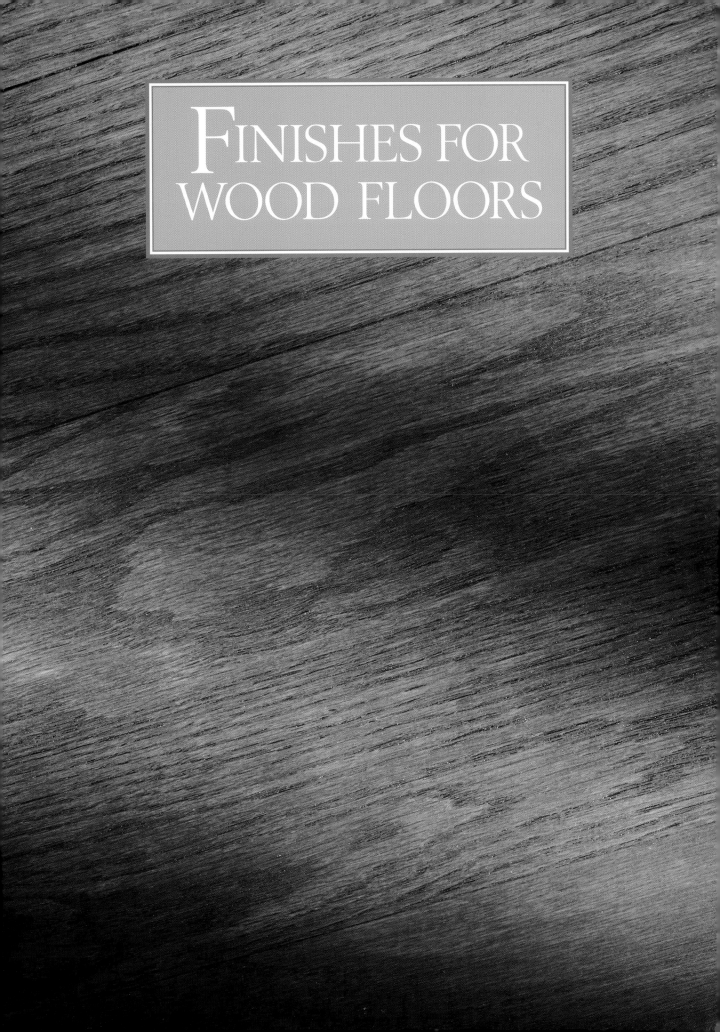

FINISHES FOR WOOD FLOORS

*R*esurfacing &
Refinishing Basics

Refinishing wood floors is one of the most popular do-it-yourself projects today, and for good reason. Few projects offer such a dramatic reward for a relatively small investment of time and money. Resurfacing may be necessary to rescue a floor that has deep scratches and uneven wear, or to remove stain or paint that has penetrated the wood grain. Because this requires power sanding (page 22), resurfacing is only possible on wood that has adequate thickness.

Many floors, however, do not need sanding but can be rejuvenated by chemically stripping (page 24) the old top coat and applying a fresh finish. A variety of stripping products are available. Some products are less toxic than others but may take longer to remove the old finish. Read labels carefully to select the products that are right for you.

Resurfacing &
Refinishing Supplies

Some specialty tools and products are necessary for resurfacing or refinishing wood floors. If many scratches, gouges, and stains have damaged the floor, it may be a good idea to resurface it by sanding, using A. a DRUM SANDER for the main floor area, and B. an EDGER SANDER for the areas next to the baseboards. Both of these tools can be rented from a home improvement or rental center. As a general rule, use the finest-grit sandpaper that is effective for the job. Be sure to get complete operating and safety instructions when renting these tools.

C. PAINT SCRAPERS are helpful for removing old finish in corners and other areas that cannot be reached by the sanders. Refinishing the floor, using D. CHEMICAL STRIPPING PRODUCTS, is often a more efficient method that yields better results. This is especially true for floors that are uneven, or for parquet and veneered floors, which must never be sanded. E. STRIPPER KNIVES and F. ABRASIVE PADS are used with the stripping products. For the final finish, G. WATER-BASED POLYURETHANE is poured into H. a PAINT TRAY and applied, using I. a wide PAINTING PAD with a pole extension.

How to resurface a wood floor

1. Countersink nails and screws so they are about ¼″ (6 mm) below floor surface; remove staples. Mask off doorways and ductwork. Vacuum floor.

2. Install 80-grit sandpaper on drum sander. Test sander on sheet of plywood before sanding floor.

3. Position the drum sander in center of the room, about 6″ (15 cm) out from the wall. With the sanding drum in raised position, turn on sander and begin moving it forward, lowering drum as the sander is moved. Sand a straight path, following direction of floorboards and keeping the sander moving constantly.

4. Complete first pass, sanding to within about 12″ (30.5 cm) of end wall; raise drum as sander nears wall. NOTE: Sander should remove most of old finish with first pass. If sandpaper clogs quickly or leaves too much finish intact, switch to coarser grit.

5. Reposition sander at starting point, over-lapping first pass by one-half its width. Make second sanding pass. Continue sanding overlapping passes up to opposite side wall. Replace sandpaper as needed. Turn sander around and sand the other half of the room.

6. Install 120-grit sandpaper. Repeat steps 3 to 5. Repeat again, using 150-grit sandpa-per, and again, using 180-grit sandpaper.

7. Sand room borders, using edger sander; use same sequence of sandpaper grits as with drum sander. When turning edger, make sure sandpaper is not resting on floor; maintain light, even pressure on sander as you work.

8. Remove finish in hard-to-reach areas, using sharp scraper or hand sander. Feather out any remaining uneven areas and sanding ridges, using finishing sander and 180-grit sandpaper.

How to chemically strip a wood floor

1. Read manufacturer's instructions for chemical stripper. Apply stripper to floor, covering area about 2' × 6' (61 × 183 cm), or the amount of space that can be scraped in the active working time of the stripper. Allow stripper to work.

2. Scrape off stripper and old finish, using nylon stripper knife; scrape in same direction as grain in floorboards. Deposit sludge on newspaper.

3. Repeat steps 1 and 2 for entire floor. Scrub floor, using medium abrasive pad dipped in mineral spirits to remove residue .

4. Clean sludge out of the gaps between floorboards, using a palette knife. Left in the gaps, these chemicals can destroy your new top coat.

5. Sand out any stains or discolorations, feathering edges of sanded area. Use bleach and oxalic acid to remove stubborn stains.

6. Touch up bare wood areas with stain in color to match the original floor stain. Allow to dry. Apply three coats of water-based polyurethane, opposite.

How to apply polyurethane to floors

1. Seal sanded wood with 1:1 mixture of water-based polyurethane and water, applied with painting pad and pole extension; allow to dry. Buff surface lightly to remove any raised wood grain, using medium abrasive pad. Vacuum surface, using bristle attachment; wipe with tack cloth.

2. Apply coat of undiluted polyurethane to floor, applying finish as evenly as possible. Do not overbrush. Allow finish to dry.

3. Buff floor with a medium abrasive pad. Vacuum floor; wipe with tack cloth. Apply more coats of polyurethane as needed to build finish to desired thickness, buffing between coats. Most floors require at least three coats of water-based polyurethane for a hard, durable finish.

4. Option: When the final coat of finish is dry, buff the surface with water and a fine abrasive pad to remove surface imperfections and diminish gloss.

Stained Floors

Stains are applied to the surface of unfinished wood floors to change the color of the wood. Or colored stains can be applied to previously stained and finished floors for a colorwashed effect. Look for a water-based stain that is formulated for easy application without lap marks or streaking. Or, if recommended by the manufacturer, use a wood conditioner on the wood prior to staining. Conditioners can help prevent streaking and help control grain raise when using water-based wood stains. Choose a stain in a natural wood tone or select a colored stain, such as green for a country decorating scheme or white for a contemporary decorating scheme.

You can also stain wood by colorwashing it with diluted latex paint. The colorwash solution will be considerably lighter in color than the original paint color. Experiment with small amounts of paint until you achieve the desired color. Use four parts water to one part paint when making a colorwash solution. Test the stain or colorwash solution in an inconspicuous area, such as a closet, to test application method and color, before staining the entire floor surface. Protect the stained floor with three coats of clear finish in satin, semi-gloss, or gloss finish. Look for a finish that is self-leveling to eliminate brush marks.

MATERIALS

- Water-based stain in desired color or latex paint.
- Synthetic brush, sponge applicator, or cotton lint-free rag, for applying stain.
- Cotton lint-free rags, for wiping stain.
- High-gloss and satin clear finishes, such as acrylic or polyurethane, for protecting stained floor.
- Sponge applicator or paint pad and pole extension, for applying clear finish.
- Fine sandpaper; tack cloth.
- Satin clear finish.

How to apply stain to a bare wood floor

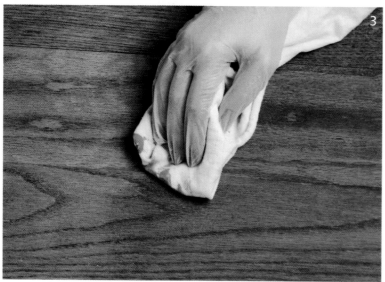

1. Sand floor surface, using fine-grit sandpaper, sanding in the direction of the wood grain. Remove sanding dust with a vacuum, if necessary; wipe with a tack cloth.

2. Stir stain or colorwash solution thoroughly. Apply stain or solution to floor, using a synthetic brush or sponge applicator, working in small sections, since stain may dry quickly; keep a wet edge and avoid overlapping.

3. Wipe away excess stain immediately or after waiting time recommended by manufacturer, using a dry lint-free rag; wipe against the grain first, then with the grain of the wood. Continue applying and wiping stain continuously until entire floor is finished. Allow stain to dry. Sand floor lightly, using fine-grit sandpaper, and remove dust particles, using a tack cloth. For deeper color, apply a second coat of stain; allow to dry thoroughly.

4. Apply a coat of high-gloss clear finish to stained floor, using a sponge applicator or paint pad with a pole extension; allow to dry. Sand floor lightly, using fine-grit sandpaper; wipe with a tack cloth. Apply two coats of satin clear finish.

COLOR EFFECTS

DARK WOOD TONES work well for traditional rooms. White colorwashing over a previously dark stained floor mellows the formal appearance.

MEDIUM, WARM WOOD TONES have a casual appearance. White colorwashing over a medium wood tone creates an antiqued look.

PALE NEUTRAL STAINS are used for contemporary rooms. A blue colorwash can give a previously pale floor bold new character.

Aged & Distressed Finishes

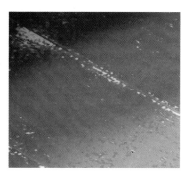

Aged finishes give floors timeworn character, making them especially suitable for a country or transitional decorating style. Though they appear distressed and fragile, these finishes are actually very durable.

Aged finishes are especially suitable for previously painted or stained floors, but may also be applied to new or resurfaced (page 19) wood flooring. Up to three coats of paint in different colors may be applied to the floor. As the floor is sanded, varying amounts of the different colors are revealed, implying that the floor had been painted different colors over time. Additional wear and stress can be simulated by pounding the floor with a hammer, chisel, or chain. Two coats of clear finish are applied to protect the distressed finish .

For previously stained and finished floors, the existing finish can also be used as the base coat. Sanding will then reveal areas of stained wood under the paint. To achieve the same look on new or resurfaced wood flooring, the wood is first stained, as on page 28, steps 2 to 4 , omitting the two coats of satin finish.

The paint colors can be selected to complement each other and blend with the desired color scheme of the room. The top coat will be the most prominent. The undercoats will show only in small amounts in the finished floor. For best results, select colors for the paint layers that have a good degree of contrast. If the floor was previously painted, it may be necessary to apply only one or two new layers of paint to the floor and use the existing layer of paint as your first coat.

MATERIALS

- Latex enamel paint in two or three contrasting colors; paint roller.
- Medium-grit sandpaper.
- Hammer, chisel, chain and awl, for distressing finish.
- Satin clear finish.

TIPS FOR PREPARING AND PAINTING WOOD FLOORING

APPLY stain-killing primer over any knotholes in new or resurfaced (page 19) wood, to seal them and prevent paint from yellowing.

APPLY clear acrylic sealer to new or resurfaced wood to prevent paint from penetrating the grain of the bare wood.

CLEAN previously painted floors with TSP to remove any wax, grease, or oil; rinse with clear water and allow to dry.

SAND the finished floor in the direction of the wood grain, using fine-grit sandpaper. Vacuum to remove dust; wipe with tack cloth.

APPLY two or three coats of latex enamel floor paint, using a roller, paintbrush, or sponge applicator. Allow to dry thoroughly between coats. Sand floor lightly between coats, using fine-grit sandpaper; wipe with tack cloth.

How to apply an aged and distressed finish

1. Follow tips, above, for finish with painted base coat. Or, for finish with stained base coat, follow steps 2 to 4 on page 28, omitting satin finish. Apply two or three coats of enamel, using a different color of paint for each coat.

2. Sand surface of floor with medium-grit sandpaper, sanding harder in some areas to remove top and middle coats of paint; avoid sanding beyond base coat of paint or stain.

3. Distress wood floor further, if desired, by hitting wood with hammer, chisel, or chain; pound holes randomly into wood, using an awl. Make as many indentations and imperfections as desired. Sand floor lightly.

4. Apply two coats of satin clear finish, allowing floor to dry completely between coats.

COLOR EFFECTS

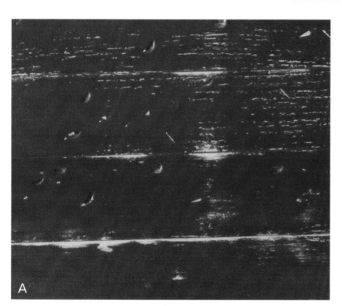

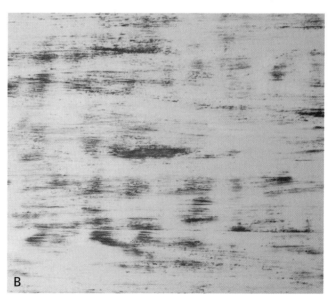

Two coats of dark green paint were applied over a previously stained floor. Sanding revealed the stain in some areas. The floor was further distressed using a hammer, chisel, and awl (A).

Maroon base coat and light rose top coat were painted over a previously stained floor. Sanding created an aged look suitable for a country bedroom (B).

Decorative Painting on Finished Floors

Painted Designs on Wood Floors

Painted designs in a variety of styles can be applied to wood floors to give the entire floor a new look, or to accent certain areas. If the floor is in poor condition, it can be camouflaged with an all-over design, such as a classic checkerboard pattern. On a smaller scale, a painted border of stripes and block-printed designs can effectively frame an attractive wood floor.

The proper preparation of the floor is essential to give long-lasting results. For a previously finished wood floor, lightly sand the areas to be painted, so the paint will adhere well to the finish. For an unfinished wood floor, prevent the paint from penetrating the grain of the bare wood by sealing it with a clear acrylic or polyurethane finish and sanding it lightly before it is painted. Be sure that the floor is free of dust before you start to paint.

Plan large designs on graph paper, and transfer the design to the floor. Use masking tape to mask off any lines for a border or geometric design. After painting the design, apply several coats of clear finish to the entire floor.

MATERIALS

- ◆ Graph paper.
- ◆ Tape measure; straightedge.
- ◆ Fine-grit sandpaper.
- ◆ Tack cloth.
- ◆ Painter's masking tape.
- ◆ Latex or acrylic paint.

- ◆ Paintbrushes.
- ◆ Closed-cell foam, wood block, felt, sheet of glass or acrylic, for block-printed designs.
- ◆ High-gloss and satin clear finishes, such as acrylic or polyurethane.

How to paint an all-over checkerboard design on a wood floor

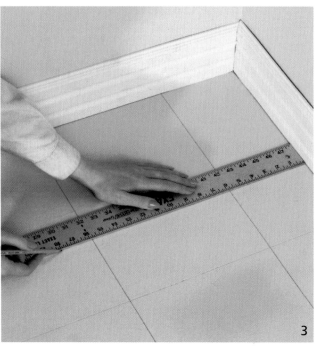

1. Sand the surface of previously stained and sealed wood floor lightly, using fine-grit sandpaper, to degloss the finish; this improves paint adhesion. Vacuum the entire floor, and wipe with tack cloth.

2. Mask off baseboards with painter's masking tape. Paint the entire floor with the lighter of the two paint colors. Allow to dry thoroughly.

3. Measure the floor. Decide on the size of squares to be used. Plan the design so that areas of the floor with the highest visibility, such as the main entrance, have full squares; place partial squares along opposite walls. Mark design lines on the floor, using a straightedge and a pencil.

4. Mask off squares that are to remain light in color, using painter's masking tape.

5. Paint the remaining squares with the darker paint color. Remove the masking tape from squares carefully before paint is completely dry.

6. Apply a coat of high-gloss clear finish, using a sponge applicator; allow to dry. Sand lightly with fine-grit sandpaper. Wipe with tack cloth. Apply two coats of satin clear finish.

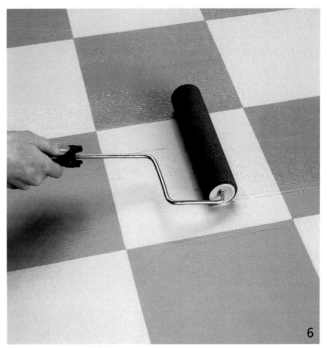

How to paint a striped border design on a wood floor

1. Sand the surface of previously stained and sealed wood floor lightly in the area to be painted, using fine-grit sandpaper, to degloss finish; this improves the paint adhesion. Vacuum the entire floor, and wipe with tack cloth.

2. Mark design lines for border on floor. Mask off stripes in design, using painter's masking tape; press firmly along the edges with a plastic credit card or your fingernail, to prevent the paint from seeping under the tape.

3. Apply paint for the stripes, using a paintbrush. Remove the masking tape. Allow the paint to dry.

4. Block-print the designs, opposite. Seal entire floor with clear finish as on page 39, step 6.

How to block-print the design

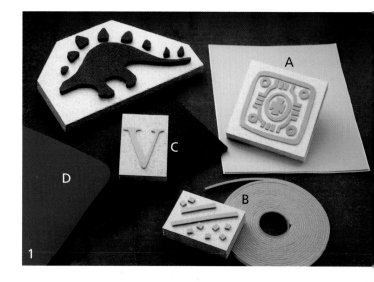

1. Make printing blocks from closed-cell foam cut to the desired shapes and attached to a wood block. Closed-cell foam is available as A. THIN, PRESSURE-SENSITIVE SHEETS, B. NEOPRENE WEATHER-STRIPPING TAPE, C. NEOPRENE SHEETS, and D. COMPUTER MOUSE PADS.

2. Thin the paint slightly with an acrylic paint extender, about three to four parts paint to one part extender. Cut a piece of felt, larger than printing block; place felt pad on glass or acrylic sheet. Pour the paint mixture onto felt, allowing paint to saturate pad.

3. Press printing block into felt pad, coating surface of foam evenly with paint.

4. Press printing block to the floor, applying firm, even pressure to the back of block. Remove the block by pulling it straight back from the floor.

How to make nature-printed designs on floors

1. Press the leaves flat by placing them between the pages of a large book for about an hour. Sand the surface of previously stained and sealed wood floor lightly in area to be printed, using fine-grit sandpaper. Wipe with tack cloth.

2. Apply thin layer of craft acrylic paint to back side of leaf, using a sponge applicator.

3. Position leaf, paint side down, over floor in desired location of print; cover with wax paper. Roll brayer over leaf to make imprint. Carefully remove wax paper and leaf.

4. Remove any unwanted paint lines from imprint, using a damp cloth before paint dries. Allow paint to dry. Repeat printing process for desired number of leaf prints. Apply two coats of clear finish over nature-printed designs.

Nature-printed Floor Designs

Use leaves to create a unique imprint on your floor. Leaves can be collected from your own backyard or can be found at the local florist. Experiment with the printing process on paper to determine which leaves provide the desired finished result. Printing with the back side of the leaf may provide more detail in the finished print.

Nature-printed designs can be applied easily over previously stained or color-washed and finished floors. A wood floor can be embellished with corner designs or a border. Or for a parquet floor, apply leaf prints randomly to the centers of the wood squares. Lightly sand the areas of the floor to be printed to ensure that the paint will adhere well to the finish. After printing the design, apply two coats of clear finish to the entire floor.

MATERIALS

- Fresh leaves, such as leatherleaf fern, salal, myrtle, or other desired leaves, for printing.
- Fine-grit sandpaper.
- Tack cloth.
- Craft acrylic paints in desired colors, for nature prints; sponge applicator.
- Wax paper.
- Rubber brayer, about 4" (10 cm) wide.
- Lint-free cloth.
- High-gloss and satin clear finishes, such as acrylic or polyurethane, for protecting nature-printed floor.
- Synthetic brush, for applying clear finish.

More ideas
for painted floors

OPPOSITE, TOP: FAUX AREA RUG, painted on the floor area under a coffee table, becomes a whimsical accessory.

OPPOSITE, BOTTOM: CHECKERS GAME BOARD is painted on the wood floor in a corner of the family room.

LEFT AND BELOW: STENCILED DESIGN is painted on a whitewashed wood floor, using precut stencils and a stencil brush.

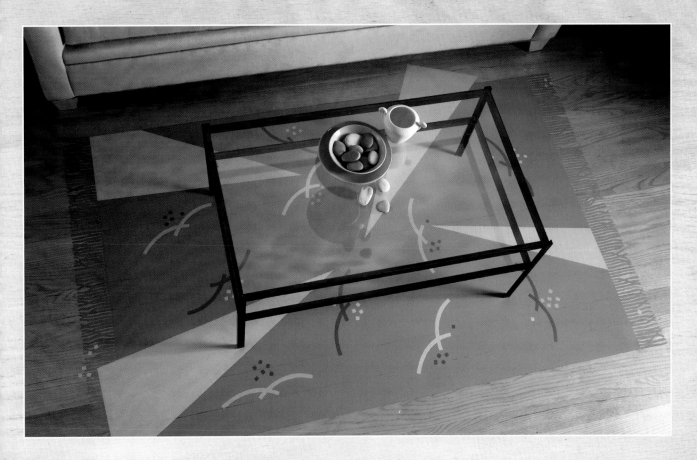

45

Faux Wood Grain

The rich patterns and colors of natural wood grain can be imitated, using a technique that dates back as far as Roman times and was especially popular in the late nineteenth century. Long revered as a technique used exclusively by skilled artisans, wood graining has made a comeback as new tools, such as the wood-graining rocker (page 48), have become available. Wood graining is suitable for any smooth surface.

For faux wood grain, a glaze of latex or craft acrylic paint and paint thickener is applied over a base coat of low-luster latex enamel. The rocker side of a wood-graining tool is dragged through the wet glaze as you rock it back and forth. Each time the tool is rocked, the oval-shaped markings characteristic of pine and other woods are simulated.

The final color of the finish depends on the combined effect of the base coat and the glaze coat. For a natural appearance of wood, a lighter base coat is used with a darker glaze. Suitable colors for the base coat include raw sienna, red oxide, burnt sienna, burnt umber, and beige tones. For the glaze, colors include burnt umber, black, red oxide, and burnt sienna. Because of the wide range of wood stains commonly used on woodwork, it is not necessary to duplicate both the grain and the color of any particular wood.

Become familiar with the techniques by practicing them on a large sheet of cardboard until you can achieve the look of wood. Test the finish before applying it to the actual project.

For the effect of wood parquet, mark the base coat in a grid, such as 4″ or 8″ (10 or 20.5 cm) squares. You can center the design, or begin at one corner with a full square. Masking off alternate squares in the gridwork, wood-grain the surface in alternating horizontal and vertical directions.

WOOD-GRAINING ROCKER

Comb edge

Reversible
handle

Rocker

Notched edge

WOOD-GRAINING GLAZE

Mix together the following ingredients:

Two parts craft acrylic paint or latex paint in desired sheen.

One part acrylic paint thickener.

MATERIALS

- Low-luster latex enamel paint in desired color, for base coat; paintbrush or paint roller.
- Craft acrylic paint in desired color or latex paint in desired sheen and color, for glaze.
- Acrylic paint thickener.
- Synthetic-bristle paintbrush, for applying glaze.

- Wood-graining rocker.
- Soft natural-bristle paintbrush, 3" or 4" (7.5 or 10 cm) wide, for blending the wood-grain effect.
- Straightedge, painter's masking tape, for faux wood parquet finish.
- Satin or high-gloss clear finish or aerosol clear acrylic sealer.

How to paint a faux wood-grain finish

1. Prepare the surface (page 10). Apply a base coat of low-luster latex enamel in the desired color, stroking in desired direction for the wood grain. A paint roller may be used for large areas. Allow to dry.

2. Mix the wood-graining glaze (above). Apply an even coat of glaze over base coat to a small area at a time, stroking in the desired direction for wood grain.

3. Slide wood-graining rocker through wet glaze, rocking it slowly to create wood-grain effect. Start at one corner, working in one continuous motion as you slide and rock the tool from one end to another. (Position of rocker corresponds to markings of wood grain, as shown opposite.)

4. Repeat step 3 for subsequent rows, varying the space between oval markings; wipe excess glaze from the tool as necessary. For some rows, pull comb or notched edge of wood-graining tool through glaze instead of using rocker; this varies the look by giving a simple, continuous wood grain.

5. Brush across surface before glaze is completely dry, using dry, soft natural-bristle paintbrush, 3" to 4" (7.5 to 10 cm) wide; lightly brush in direction of wood grain, to soften the look. Wipe excess glaze from brush as necessary. Allow the glaze to dry. Apply clear finish or aerosol clear acrylic sealer, if desired.

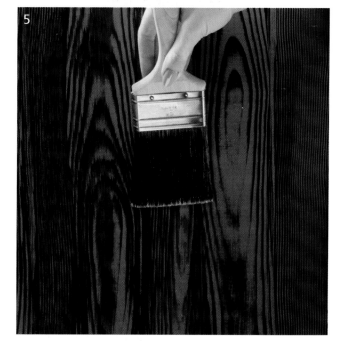

How to apply a faux wood parquet finish

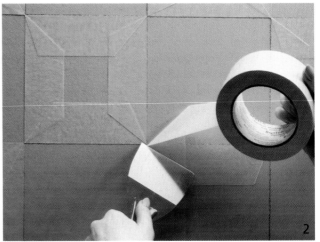

1. Apply a base coat as on page 48, step 1. Measure and mark grid on base coat, using straightedge and pencil; center grid or begin with a complete square at one corner.

2. Apply painter's masking tape to alternate squares in grid; use putty knife to trim masking tape diagonally at corners, as shown. Press firmly along the edges of tape, to prevent glaze from seeping through.

3. Mix the wood-graining glaze (page 48). Apply glaze to unmasked squares, using paintbrush in horizontal direction. Slide wood-graining rocker horizontally through wet glaze on some squares for straight wood-grain effect. Rock the tool horizontally on

remaining squares, varying position of oval markings. Work on only a few squares at a time, because glaze dries quickly.

4. Brush across the surface before glaze is completely dry, using dry, soft, natural-bristle paintbrush; lightly brush in direction of wood grain, to soften it. Wipe excess glaze from brush as necessary.

5. Allow paint to dry; remove the masking tape. Apply masking tape over wood-grained squares; apply glaze to unmasked squares, brushing in a vertical direction. Repeat steps 3 and 4 in vertical direction. Allow to dry; remove masking tape. Apply clear finish or aerosol clear acrylic sealer, if desired.

COLOR EFFECTS

Various wood tones, resembling common wood stains such as cherry, honey oak, and walnut, can be created, depending on the paint colors selected for the base coat and the glaze.

Cherry stain is duplicated by using a dark rust base coat and a burnt umber glaze (A).

Honey oak is duplicated by using a light tan base coat and a golden tan glaze (B).

Walnut stain is duplicated by using a dark gold base coat and a burnt umber glaze (C).

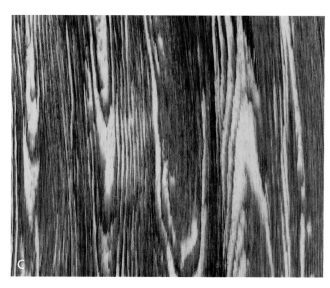

*F*aux Stone Tiles

A painted finish that mimics unpolished stone can be applied to a floor, using newspaper instead of paintbrushes or special tools. Rustic grout lines in the finish create the look of expensive stone tiles.

A variety of earth-tone glazes can be combined to make a stone finish in the color desired. In general, only two or three colors need to be used, because they will blend together and develop a range of tones as the finish is applied.

To create the grout lines, masking tape is applied to the surface in a grid, but not burnished. This allows some of the paint to seep under the tape edges, creating a slightly rough line. After the faux finish is applied, the tape is removed and the grout is painted in by hand, without caution or accuracy, thus creating the rustic look.

MATERIALS

- ¼" (6 mm) masking tape.
- White low-luster latex enamel paint, for base coat; sponge or low-napped roller.
- Flat paint glazes in a variety of earth-tone colors, black, and white.
- Newspapers.

- White wash; earth-tone wash; cheesecloth.
- Matte clear finish or aerosol matte clear acrylic sealer, optional.
- Round artist's brush.
- Glaze in shade to contrast with faux finish.

How to apply a faux unpolished stone finish using the newspaper method

1. Prepare the surface (page 10). Apply base coat of white low-luster latex enamel. Allow to dry. Mask off grout lines, opposite, if desired.

2. Apply flat earth-tone glaze in random strokes; repeat with another color. Apply white wash in areas desired; apply earth-tone wash in areas desired.

3. Fold a sheet of newspaper to several layers. Lay it flat over one area of surface and press into glaze. Lift, removing some glaze. Repeat in other areas, turning same newspaper in different directions to blend colors roughly.

4. Add more color to an area by spreading glaze on newspaper and laying it flat on surface. Repeat as necessary until desired effect is achieved. Leave some dark accent areas in finish; also leave an occasional light spot. Use same newspaper throughout. Allow to dry.

5. Apply white wash to entire surface. Dab with wadded cheesecloth to soften. Allow to dry. Apply matte clear finish or aerosol matte clear acrylic sealer, if desired.

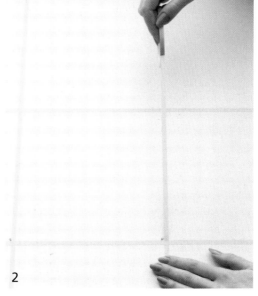

How to apply
rustic grout lines

1. Plan placement of grout lines; mark points of intersections on floor, using a pencil.

2. Stretch ¼" (6 mm) masking tape taut; apply to surface in horizontal lines, positioning tape just under marked points. Repeat for vertical lines, positioning tapes just to right of marks. Press tapes firmly in place with pads of fingers; do not burnish.

3. Apply desired faux finish. Allow to dry. Remove tapes.

4. Paint over the grout lines freehand, using round artist's brush and desired glaze to contrast with faux finish. Allow lines to have some irregularity in thickness and density. Allow to dry. Apply finish or sealer to the entire surface as desired.

Floor Cloths

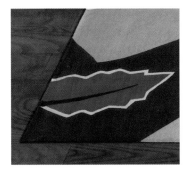

Express your creativity by making a custom floor cloth with decorative painting or stenciling. Used at the entryway to the living room or as an area rug, a floor cloth can become an artwork conversation piece.

When designing the floor cloth, you may want to browse through art books or quilt books for design ideas and use a photocopy machine to enlarge the design to the desired size. Or duplicate a design used elsewhere in the room, such as a fabric or wallpaper design. For a perfect color match, have the paint colors for the floor cloth custom-mixed to match the fabric or wallpaper swatches.

An 18-ounce (500 gram) or #8 canvas provides a durable surface for floor cloths and lies flat on the floor. It is available in widths up to 5 feet (152.5 centimeters) at tent and awning stores and upholstery shops.

Paint the canvas, using latex paints intended for floors and patios. These paints are very durable and can be custom-mixed by the quart (0.9 liter). Or stencil the canvas, using oil-based paint crayons designed for stenciling; this type of paint will not bleed when applied to the fabric. To protect the floor cloth from abrasion, seal it with a nonyellowing latex urethane acrylic finish.

If the rug will be placed on a smooth floor surface, such as linoleum or ceramic, place a nonslip pad under the floor cloth.

How to make a painted floor cloth

MATERIALS

- 18-oz. (500 g) or #8 canvas.

- Latex floor paints in desired colors, paint roller, roller tray, and paintbrushes, for painted floor cloth.

- Oil-based paint crayons and stencil brushes, for stenciled floor cloth.

- Sealer, such as a nonyellowing latex urethane acrylic finish.

- Synthetic-bristle paintbrush, for applying sealer.

- Plastic drop cloth; carpenter's square; straightedge.

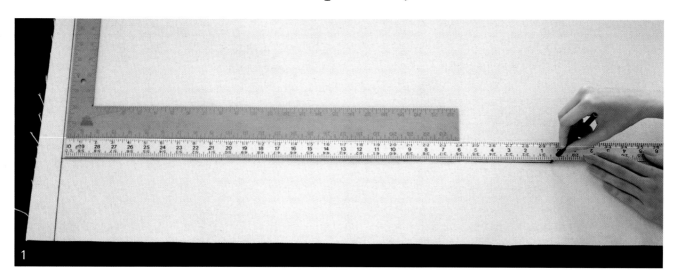

1. Trim selvages from canvas. Mark canvas to desired size, using pencil, carpenter's square, and straightedge; cut canvas.

2. Machine-stitch around the canvas 1/4" (6 mm) from raw edges; stitch a second row of stitching 1/8" (3 mm) from raw edges. Press canvas so it lies flat.

3. Place canvas on a plastic drop cloth. Using paint roller, apply background color of paint, taking care not to crease canvas; roll paint in all directions to penetrate fabric. Allow to dry. Apply additional coats as necessary; allow to dry overnight. Trim any loose threads.

4. Mark design, if desired, using pencil. Paint desired design, applying one color at a time. Use a fine-pointed brush for outlining and wider brush for filling in design areas. Allow paint to dry 24 hours.

5. Apply sealer, using synthetic-bristle paintbrush; allow to dry several hours. Apply two additional coats of sealer, following manufacturer's instructions for drying time.

STENCILED FLOOR CLOTH. Prepare the canvas as in steps 1 and 2, opposite. Apply background color as in step 3, if desired. Stencil design, using paint crayons. Apply sealer as in step 5, above.

More ideas for painted floor cloths

OPPOSITE, TOP: QUILT DESIGN has been enlarged for
this floor cloth.

OPPOSITE, BOTTOM: STENCILED FLOOR CLOTH
echoes the design applied to the walls.

BELOW: GEOMETRIC FABRIC DESIGN was mimicked
to create a coordinating floor cloth.

Index

A

Aerosol clear acrylic sealer, 13

Aged and distressed finishes, 31-33

Applicators and paintbrushes, 9

B

Border design,

    block-printed, 41

    striped, painting on a wood floor, 40

Brush combs, 9

Brushes, for painting, 9

C

Checkerboard design, painting on a wood floor, 38-39

Checkers game board design for finished wood floor, 44

Chemically stripping a wood floor, 24

Clear finish, 13

Cloths, floor, painted, 57-61

Craft acrylic paint, 15

D

Decorative painting on finished floors,

    faux stone tiles, 53-55

    faux wood grain, 47-51

    floor cloths, 57-61

    nature-printed floor design, 42-43

    painted designs on wood floors, 37-41

Designs for finished wood floors,

    block-print, 41

    checkerboard, 38-39

    checkers game board, 44

    faux area rug, 44

    nature-printed, 42-43

    stenciled, 44

    striped border, 40

Distressed and aged finishes, 31-33

E

Edgers, paint, 9

Extension pole, paint rollers, 8

F

Faux area rug design for finished wood floor, 44

Faux stone tiles, 53-55

Faux wood grain, 47-51

Finishes, 13

Finishes for wood floors,

    see: Wood floors, finishes for

Flat latex primer, 11-12

Floor cloths, painted, 57-61

Frame, roller, 8

G

Grout lines, rustic, 55

L

Latex enamel undercoat, 11-12

Latex paints, 14

N

Nature-printed floor designs, 42-43

P

Pads, roller, 8

Paintbrushes and applicators, 9

Painted designs on wood floors, 37-41

Paint edgers, 9

Paint rollers, 8

Paint scrapers, 21

Paints, water-based, 14-15

Parquet finish, faux wood, 50

Polyurethane, applying to floors, 25

Preparing surface, 10-11

Primers, 11-12

R

Refinishing, 22-25

   basics, 19

   supplies, 20-21

Resurfacing, 22-25

   basics, 19

   supplies, 20-21

Rocker, wood-graining, 48

Roller frame, 8

Roller pads, 8

Rollers, paint, 8

S

Sanders, 20

Scrapers, paint, 21

Sealer, aerosol clear acrylic, 13

Sponge applicators, 9

Stained floors, 27-29

Stain-killing primer, 11-12

Stains, water-based, 15

Stenciled design for finished wood floor, 44

Stone tiles, faux, 53-55

Striped border design, painting on a wood floor, 40

Stripping wood floors, chemically, 24

Supplies and tools, 8-9

   resurfacing and refinishing, 20-21

Surfaces, preparing, 10-11

T

Tapes, 8

Tools and supplies, 8-9

   resurfacing and refinishing, 20-21

U

Undercoat, latex enamel, 11-12

W

Water-based paints and stains, 14-15

Wood floors, finishes for,

   aged and distressed finishes, 31-33

   resurfacing and refinishing, 19-25

   stained floors, 27-29

Wood-grain finish, faux, 47-51

Wood-graining rocker, 48

COWLES Creative Publishing

A Division of Cowles Enthusiast Media, Inc.

President/COO: Nino Tarantino
Executive V.P./Editor-in-Chief: William B. Jones

Creative Touches™
Group Executive Editor: Zoe A. Graul
Managing Editor: Elaine Johnson
Editor: Linda Neubauer
Associate Creative Director: Lisa Rosenthal
Senior Art Director: Delores Swanson
Art Director: Mark Jacobson
Copy Editor: Janice Cauley
Desktop Publishing Specialist: Laurie Kristensen
Photo Studio Services Manager: Marcia Chambers
Print Production Manager: Patt Sizer

COWLES Enthusiast Media

President/COO: Philip L. Penny

FLOOR FINISHES ETC.
Created by: The Editors of Cowles Creative Publishing, Inc.

Floor finishes etc.
    p. cm. -- (Creative touches)
  Includes index.
  ISBN 0-86573-878-5 (softcover)
  1. Wood finishing -- Amateurs' manuals. 2. Floors, Wooden -
-Amateurs' manuals. 3. House painting -- Amateurs' manuals.
4. Interior decoration--Amateurs' manuals.   I. Cowles Creative
Publishing. II. Series.
TT325.F56 1997   96-37444
698'. 146 -- dc21   CIP

Books available in the Creative Touches™ series:

*Stenciling Etc., Sponging Etc., Stone Finishes Etc., Valances Etc.,
Painted Designs Etc., Metallic Finishes Etc., Swags Etc.,
Papering Projects Etc., Wall Finishes Etc., Floor Finishes Etc.*

The Creative Touches™ series draws from the individual titles of
The Home Decorating Institute®. Individual titles are also available
from the publisher and in bookstores and fabric stores.

Printed on American paper by:
  R. R. Donnelley & Sons Co.
99 98 97 96 / 5 4 3 2 1

Cowles Creative Publishing, Inc. offers a variety of how-to books.
For information write:
  Cowles Creative Publishing
    Subscriber Books
  5900 Green Oak Drive
  Minnetonka, MN 55343